THE RISEN CHRIST

We proclaim your Death,
O Lord,
and profess your Resurrection
until you come again.

This Book Belongs to

....

who first became a child of God and shared in His life in Baptism on

....

Date of Baptism

---

who first confessed sins to the Priest to receive God's forgiveness on

....

Date of First Penance

---

who was nourished by the Body and Blood of Jesus for the first time on

....

Date of First Holy Communion

At the Last Supper, Jesus changed bread and wine into His Body and Blood. This was the first Holy Mass. Then Jesus said to His Apostles, "Do this in memory of me."

New... Saint Joseph

CHILDREN'S MISSAL

A Helpful Way to Participate at Mass

With Official Text of People's Parts of the Holy Mass Printed in Bold Type

In Accord with the Third Typical Edition of *The Roman Missal*

CATHOLIC BOOK PUBLISHING CORP.
New Jersey

Dear Children:

THIS is your own Missal. Take it with you when you go to Mass. It will help you to adore God and thank Him, to praise and love Him.

On many pages of the Mass section of this book, you will find a picture. The picture will show you what the Priest is doing. The accompanying prayer will help you to pray with the Priest and people throughout the Mass. The words in heavy black type are said aloud by everyone.

Using this Missal will help you to take a more active part at every Mass.

NIHIL OBSTAT: Rev. Pawel Tomczyk, Ph.D.
Censor Librorum

IMPRIMATUR: ✠ Arthur J. Serratelli, S.T.D., S.S.L., D.D.
Bishop of Paterson

December 16, 2019

The publishers wish to thank Rev. Stephen Prisk and the students of St. Anthony School for their great help in the publication of this book.

(T-806)

Printed in China

CPSIA November 2022 10 9 8 7 6 5 4 3 L/P

HOLY MASS

ON THE CROSS Christ offered His Body and Blood to God the Father for us. In the Mass this great act is repeated.

Mass begins with the *Introductory Rites* (page 11). We speak to God in acts of contrition, praise, and petition.

Then follows the *Liturgy of the Word* (page 21). We listen to what God says to us in the Readings, the Gospel, and the Homily.

The *Liturgy of the Eucharist* (page 30), has three parts.

(1) With the Priest we present the gifts of bread and wine (*Presentation and Preparation of the Gifts*, page 30).

(2) At the consecration this bread and wine are changed into the Body and Blood of Christ (*Eucharistic Prayer*, page 35).

(3) In Holy Communion we receive Christ who has given Himself in love (*Communion Rite*, page 51).

Mass ends with the Blessing and the Dismissal (*Concluding Rites*, page 61).

We sing hymns to praise God and to show our joy at Mass.

1
2
3
4
5
6
7
8
9
10
10

THINGS I SEE AT THE ALTAR

1. The **ALTAR** is a holy table used for Mass.

2. The **CRUETS** contain the wine and water to be used at the Preparation of the Gifts.

3. The **CHALICE** is a cup that holds Our Lord's Precious Blood at Mass.

4. The **CIBORIUM** is a cup with a cover that holds the Hosts the people receive at Communion.

5. The **MONSTRANCE** is where Our Lord's Body is placed so people can see and adore Him.

6. The **TABERNACLE** holds consecrated Hosts.

7. The **CRUCIFIX** is a cross with a likeness of Our Lord's Body on it. It reminds us He died for us because He loves us.

8. The **PATEN**, or plate, holds the bread to be consecrated by the Priest.

9. The **MISSAL** is a big book with the prayers of the Mass. It often rests on a stand on the altar.

10. The **CANDLES** remind us of Our Lord. They are made of pure wax. They burn like His Sacred Heart.

ENTRANCE PROCESSION — Mass begins with an Entrance Chant during which the Priest and his ministers come to the altar.

THE ORDER OF MASS

THE INTRODUCTORY RITES

STAND

♩ ♪ ♪ ENTRANCE CHANT ♪ ♪ ♩

All make the Sign of the Cross:

PRIEST: In the name of the Father, and of the Son, and of the Holy Spirit.

PEOPLE: **Amen.**

THE GREETING

One of the following forms is used:
(Shown by A, B, or C)

A

PRIEST: The grace of our Lord Jesus Christ,
and the love of God,
and the communion of the Holy Spirit
be with you all.

PEOPLE: **And with your spirit.**

KISSING THE ALTAR — After the entrance procession, the Priest shows reverence for the altar, symbol of Christ, with a kiss. Then he says the Greeting.

OR

B

PRIEST: Grace to you and peace from God our Father
and the Lord Jesus Christ.

PEOPLE: **And with your spirit.**

OR

C

PRIEST: The Lord be with you.

PEOPLE: **And with your spirit.**

THE PENITENTIAL ACT

PRIEST: Brethren (brothers and sisters),
let us acknowledge our sins,
and so prepare ourselves to celebrate the sacred mysteries.

Then one of the following forms is used.

A

PRIEST and **PEOPLE:**

I confess to almighty God
and to you, my brothers and sisters,
that I have greatly sinned,
in my thoughts and in my words,
in what I have done and in what I have failed to do,

And, striking their breast, they say:

through my fault, through my fault,
through my most grievous fault;

Then they continue:

therefore I ask blessed Mary ever-Virgin,
all the Angels and Saints,
and you, my brothers and sisters,
to pray for me to the Lord our God.

OR

B

PRIEST: Have mercy on us, O Lord.

PEOPLE: **For we have sinned against you.**

PRIEST: Show us, O Lord, your mercy.

PEOPLE: **And grant us your salvation.**

OR

C

PRIEST or other minister:
You were sent to heal the contrite of heart:
Lord, have mercy.

PEOPLE: **Lord, have mercy.**

PRIEST or other minister:
You came to call sinners:
Christ, have mercy.

PEOPLE: **Christ, have mercy.**

PRIEST or other minister:
You are seated at the right hand of the Father to intercede for us:
Lord, have mercy.

PEOPLE: **Lord, have mercy.**

(Other invocations may be used.)

At the end of any of the forms of the Penitential Act is said:

PRIEST: May almighty God have mercy on us,
forgive us our sins,
and bring us to everlasting life.

PEOPLE: **Amen.**

THE KYRIE

Unless it is included in the Penitential Act, the Kyrie is sung or said by the people with the choir or cantor.

℣. Lord, have mercy.

℟. **Lord, have mercy.**

℣. Christ, have mercy.

℟. **Christ, have mercy.**

℣. Lord, have mercy.

℟. **Lord, have mercy.**

THE GLORIA — We praise God by recalling the words sung by the Angels when Jesus was born.

THE GLORIA

When the Gloria is sung or said the Priest or everyone together may say:

**Glory to God in the highest,
and on earth peace to people of good will.**

**We praise you,
we bless you,
we adore you,
we glorify you,
we give you thanks for your great glory,
Lord God, heavenly King,
O God, almighty Father.**

**Lord Jesus Christ, Only Begotten Son,
Lord God, Lamb of God, Son of the Father,
you take away the sins of the world,
have mercy on us;
you take away the sins of the world,
receive our prayer;
you are seated at the right hand of the Father,
have mercy on us.**

**For you alone are the Holy One,
you alone are the Lord,
you alone are the Most High,
Jesus Christ,
with the Holy Spirit,
in the glory of God the Father. Amen.**

THE COLLECT — We join with the Priest silently as he prays aloud for all people.

THE COLLECT

PRIEST: Let us pray.

Priest and people pray silently for a while.

Then the Priest says the Collect, which gives the theme of the particular celebration and asks God to help us.

The Collect often concludes with:

Through our Lord Jesus Christ, your Son,
who lives and reigns with you in the unity of the Holy Spirit,
God, for ever and ever.

PEOPLE: Amen.

THE FIRST READING — We listen to the reader who proclaims God's Word.

Liturgy of the Word

SIT

THE FIRST READING

God Speaks to Us through the Prophets

We sit and listen to the Word of God as it was spoken through His Prophets and Apostles. The reader takes their place in speaking to us.

At the end of the reading:

READER: The word of the Lord.

PEOPLE: Thanks be to God.

RESPONSORIAL PSALM — We recite or sing a part of a Psalm to show that we accept God's Word, which was just read.

RESPONSORIAL PSALM

The people repeat the response sung by the cantor or said by the reader the first time and then after each verse.

Then follows:

THE SECOND READING

God Speaks to Us through the Apostles

At the end of the reading:

READER: The word of the Lord.

PEOPLE: Thanks be to God.

Jesus will speak to us in the Gospel. We rise now out of respect and prepare for His message with the Alleluia.

STAND

ALLELUIA

The people repeat the Alleluia after the cantor's or the reader's Alleluia and then after the verse.

THE GOSPEL — The Priest now reads the Gospel in the name of Jesus, and Jesus Himself becomes present among us through His Word.

THE GOSPEL

STAND

DEACON (or Priest):
The Lord be with you.

PEOPLE: **And with your spirit.**

DEACON (or Priest):

✠ A reading from the holy Gospel according to N.

PEOPLE: **Glory to you, O Lord.**

We listen to the Priest or Deacon proclaim the Word of God.

At the end the Deacon (or Priest) says:

The Gospel of the Lord.

PEOPLE: **Praise to you, Lord Jesus Christ.**

THE HOMILY

SIT

God Speaks to Us through the Priest

The Homily helps us to put the words of Christ into practice.

PROFESSION OF FAITH — I tell God I believe all that He has taught me.

THE PROFESSION OF FAITH

STAND

I believe in one God,
the Father almighty,
maker of heaven and earth,
of all things visible and invisible.

I believe in one Lord Jesus Christ,
the Only Begotten Son of God,
born of the Father before all ages.
God from God, Light from Light,
true God from true God,
begotten, not made, consubstantial with the Father;
through him all things were made.
For us men and for our salvation
he came down from heaven,

At the words that follow, up to and including and became man, *all bow.*

and by the Holy Spirit was incarnate of the Virgin Mary,
and became man.

For our sake he was crucified under Pontius Pilate,
he suffered death and was buried,
and rose again on the third day
in accordance with the Scriptures.
He ascended into heaven
and is seated at the right hand of the Father.

He will come again in glory
to judge the living and the dead
and his kingdom will have no end.

I believe in the Holy Spirit, the Lord, the giver of life,
who proceeds from the Father and the Son,
who with the Father and the Son is adored and glorified,
who has spoken through the prophets.

I believe in one, holy, catholic and apostolic Church.
I confess one Baptism for the forgiveness of sins
and I look forward to the resurrection of the dead
and the life of the world to come. Amen.

In celebrations of Masses with Children, the Apostles' Creed, page 97, may replace the Profession of Faith given above.

UNIVERSAL PRAYER — We unite with one another to pray for the needs of our community, the whole Church, and all people.

PEOPLE: Lord, hear our prayer.

(or other response)

At the end the Priest says the concluding prayer.

PEOPLE: Amen.

PRESENTATION AND PREPARATION OF THE GIFTS

OFFERTORY CHANT — While the gifts of the people are brought forward to the Priest and are placed on the altar, the Offertory Chant is sung.

PREPARATION OF THE BREAD — The Priest thanks God for giving us the bread that will soon be changed into Christ's Body. The Priest says quietly:

Blessed are you, Lord God of all creation,
for through your goodness we have received
the bread we offer you:
fruit of the earth and work of human hands,
it will become for us the bread of life.

If there is no singing, the response is:

PEOPLE: Blessed be God for ever.

PREPARATION OF THE WINE — The Priest thanks God for giving us the wine that will be changed into Christ's Blood.

Blessed are you, Lord God of all creation,
for through your goodness we have received the wine we offer you:
fruit of the vine and work of human hands,
it will become our spiritual drink.

If there is no singing, the response is:

PEOPLE: Blessed be God for ever.

INVITATION TO PRAYER

PRIEST: Pray, brethren (brothers and sisters),
that my sacrifice and yours
may be acceptable to God,
the almighty Father.

PEOPLE: **May the Lord accept the sacrifice at your hands**
for the praise and glory of his name,
for our good
and the good of all his holy Church.

PRAYER OVER THE OFFERINGS

STAND

We Ask God to Accept Our Offerings

At the end of the Priest's Prayer over the Offerings:

PEOPLE: **Amen.**

PREFACE DIALOGUE — The Priest invites us to join with him in the words he addresses to the Father through Jesus.

EUCHARISTIC PRAYER

PREFACE DIALOGUE

PRIEST: The Lord be with you.

PEOPLE: **And with your spirit.**

PRIEST: Lift up your hearts.

PEOPLE: **We lift them up to the Lord.**

PRIEST: Let us give thanks to the Lord our God.

PEOPLE: **It is right and just.**

THE PREFACE — The Priest begins with a prayer of praise to God for the great works He has done for us in Jesus.

THE PREFACE

Our Prayer of Thanksgiving

Praise to the Father

It is truly right and just, our duty and our salvation,
always and everywhere to give you thanks, Father most holy,
through your beloved Son, Jesus Christ,
your Word through whom you made all things,
whom you sent as our Savior and Redeemer,
incarnate by the Holy Spirit and born of the Virgin.

Fulfilling your will and gaining for you a holy people,
he stretched out his hands as he endured his Passion,
so as to break the bonds of death and manifest the resurrection.

And so, with the Angels and all the Saints,
we declare your glory,
as with one voice we acclaim:

THE "HOLY, HOLY, HOLY"

First Acclamation of the People

PRIEST and **PEOPLE:**

Holy, Holy, Holy Lord God of hosts.
Heaven and earth are full of your glory.
Hosanna in the highest.
Blessed is he who comes in the name of the Lord.
Hosanna in the highest.

KNEEL

THE "HOLY, HOLY, HOLY" — We join with the Priest and the Angels to praise God the Father and Jesus Whom He has sent.

Invocation of the Holy Spirit

You are indeed Holy, O Lord,
the fount of all holiness.
Make holy, therefore, these gifts, we pray,
by sending down your Spirit upon them like the dewfall,
so that they may become for us
the Body and ✠ Blood of our Lord Jesus Christ.

The Lord's Supper

At the time he was betrayed
and entered willingly into his Passion,
he took bread and, giving thanks, broke it,
and gave it to his disciples, saying:

Take this, all of you, and eat of it,
for this is my Body,
which will be given up for you.

ELEVATION OF THE HOST — The Priest shows the consecrated Host to the people, places it again on the paten, and genuflects in adoration.

In a similar way, when supper was ended,
he took the chalice
and, once more giving thanks,
he gave it to his disciples, saying:

Take this, all of you, and drink from it,
for this is the chalice of my Blood,
the Blood of the new and eternal covenant,
which will be poured out for you and for many
for the forgiveness of sins.

Do this in memory of me.

ELEVATION OF THE CHALICE — The Priest shows the chalice to the people, places it on the corporal, and genuflects in adoration.

PRIEST: The mystery of faith.

PEOPLE:

A

We proclaim your Death, O Lord,
and profess your Resurrection
until you come again.

OR

B

When we eat this Bread and drink this Cup,
we proclaim your Death, O Lord,
until you come again.

OR

C

Save us, Savior of the world,
for by your Cross and Resurrection
you have set us free.

The Memorial Prayer

Therefore, as we celebrate
the memorial of his Death and Resurrection,
we offer you, Lord,
the Bread of life and the Chalice of salvation,
giving thanks that you have held us worthy
to be in your presence and minister to you.

Invocation of the Holy Spirit

Humbly we pray
that, partaking of the Body and Blood of Christ,
we may be gathered into one by the Holy Spirit.

Intercessions: For the Church

Remember, Lord, your Church,
spread throughout the world,
and bring her to the fullness of charity,
together with N. our Pope and N. our Bishop
and all the clergy.

THE INTERCESSIONS — The Priest prays for all the members of the Church — those who are still alive and those who have died.

For the Dead

Remember also our brothers and sisters
who have fallen asleep in the hope of the resurrection,
and all who have died in your mercy:
welcome them into the light of your face.

In Communion with the Saints

Have mercy on us all, we pray,
that with the Blessed Virgin Mary, Mother of God,
with blessed Joseph, her Spouse,
with the blessed Apostles,
and all the Saints who have pleased you throughout the ages,
we may merit to be coheirs to eternal life,
and may praise and glorify you
through your Son, Jesus Christ.

Through him, and with him, and in him,
O God, almighty Father,
in the unity of the Holy Spirit,
all glory and honor is yours,
for ever and ever.

PEOPLE: **Amen.**

END OF EUCHARISTIC PRAYER — Lifting up the Host and chalice, the Priest gives glory to God through Jesus. We join him as we acclaim: AMEN.

THE LORD'S PRAYER — Our preparation for a very close union with Jesus in Holy Communion begins with the "Our Father," the prayer that Jesus taught us to say.

THE LORD'S PRAYER

PRIEST: At the Savior's command
and formed by divine teaching,
we dare to say: **STAND**

PRIEST and **PEOPLE:**

**Our Father, who art in heaven,
hallowed be thy name;
thy kingdom come,
thy will be done
on earth as it is in heaven.
Give us this day our daily bread,
and forgive us our trespasses,
as we forgive those who trespass against us;
and lead us not into temptation,
but deliver us from evil.**

PRIEST: Deliver us, Lord, we pray, from every evil,
graciously grant peace in our days,
that, by the help of your mercy,
we may be always free from sin
and safe from all distress,
as we await the blessed hope
and the coming of our Savior, Jesus Christ.

PEOPLE: **For the kingdom,
the power and the glory are yours
now and for ever.**

SIGN OF PEACE

The Priest says the prayer for peace:

PRIEST: Lord Jesus Christ,
who said to your Apostles:
Peace I leave you, my peace I give you,
look not on our sins,
but on the faith of your Church,
and graciously grant her peace and unity
in accordance with your will.
Who live and reign for ever and ever.

PEOPLE: **Amen.**

PRIEST: The peace of the Lord be with you always.

PEOPLE: **And with your spirit.**

PRIEST: Let us offer each other the sign of peace.

SIGN OF PEACE — At this time, we exchange a sign that expresses peace, communion, and charity, in keeping with local customs.

BREAKING OF THE BREAD — The Priest breaks the bread, showing that we must all share of the one Body Who is Christ.

BREAKING OF THE BREAD

The people sing or say:

Lamb of God, you take away the sins of the world,
have mercy on us.
Lamb of God, you take away the sins of the world,
have mercy on us.
Lamb of God, you take away the sins of the world,
grant us peace.

PRAYER BEFORE COMMUNION — The Priest invites us to receive Jesus, our Savior, Who comes to us in Communion.

PRIEST: Behold the Lamb of God,
behold him who takes away the sins of the world.
Blessed are those called to the supper of the Lamb.

COMMUNION OF THE PRIEST — The Priest prays with us, asking God to make us worthy to receive Him.

PRIEST and **PEOPLE:**

Lord, I am not worthy
that you should enter under my roof,
but only say the word
and my soul shall be healed.

He then receives Communion.

COMMUNION OF THE PEOPLE — As the Priest shows us the Host, we express our faith that we are receiving Jesus, the Lord.

PRIEST: The Body of Christ.

PEOPLE: Amen.

♩ ♪ ♩ COMMUNION CHANT ♩ ♪ ♩

The Communion Chant is sung while Communion is given to the faithful.

SIT

SILENCE AFTER COMMUNION

After Communion there may be a period of silence, or a song of praise may be sung.

PRAYER AFTER COMMUNION

STAND

PRIEST: Let us pray.

Priest and people may pray silently for a while. Then the Priest says the Prayer after Communion.

At the end:

PRIEST: Through Christ our Lord.

PEOPLE: Amen.

THE BLESSING — Before ending the celebration, the Priest gives us God's blessing.

THE CONCLUDING RITES

We have heard God's Word and eaten the Body of Christ. Now it is time for us to leave, to do good works, to praise and bless the Lord in our daily lives.

After any brief announcements (sit), the Blessing and Dismissal follow:

THE BLESSING

STAND

PRIEST: The Lord be with you.

PEOPLE: **And with your spirit.**

PRIEST: May almighty God bless you, the Father, and the Son, ✠ and the Holy Spirit.

PEOPLE: **Amen.**

DISMISSAL

DEACON (or Priest):

A Go forth, the Mass is ended.

B Go and announce the Gospel of the Lord.

C Go in peace, glorifying the Lord by your life.

D Go in peace.

PEOPLE: **Thanks be to God.**

RECESSIONAL — The Priest dismisses us and we go home to live as good Christians.

JESUS CHRIST,
Our Lord and Savior

The LIFE OF CHRIST IN PICTURES

✠

Each Sunday and feastday Mass contains parts that change in accord with the particular mystery of Christ's life. In this way, the prayers at Mass recall for us the Life, Death, Resurrection, and Ascension of Jesus.

This section will help you to know our Lord's life better, so that you can take a more active part at every Mass during the year.

THE ANNUNCIATION — God sends the Angel Gabriel to the Virgin Mary. He says that she will bear a son by the power of the Holy Spirit. She is to name Him Jesus. He will be called the Son of God.

THE VISITATION — Mary visits her cousin Elizabeth. Elizabeth praises Mary's great faith and calls her "blessed among women."

JESUS IS BORN — Jesus is born in a stable because there is no room for Him and His Mother Mary and Joseph at the local inn.

VISIT OF THE WISE MEN — Wise Men from the East come to Jerusalem to learn where the newborn King of the Jews is. Finding Jesus, they kneel down to worship Him.

THE NAME JESUS — Eight days after His Birth, Mary's Son is named Jesus. This name means that He came to save us from our sins and lead us to heaven.

JESUS WITH JOSEPH — When Jesus is old enough, He helps Joseph in the carpenter shop. He works there until He is about 30 to support His Mother.

JESUS IN THE TEMPLE — At the age of twelve Jesus becomes separated from His parents for three days. They find Him in the Temple with the teachers.

THE BAPTISM OF JESUS — John baptizes Jesus in the Jordan River. Then the heavens open, and the Spirit of God appears. God declares that Jesus is His Son.

JESUS IS TEMPTED — In the desert, the devil tries to have Jesus do something wrong. Jesus refuses and drives the Evil One away.

JESUS CALLS HIS FIRST APOSTLES — Jesus simply says, "Come, follow Me" to fishermen Peter and Andrew, and they follow Him. Two other fishermen, James and John, do the same.

JESUS CHANGES WATER INTO WINE — When the wine runs out at a marriage feast, Mary asks Jesus to help. He has six jars filled with water. When the headwaiter tastes it, it has become wine.

JESUS WANTS GOOD DEEDS — Jesus tells His disciples that a good tree bears good fruit. In the same way, good people do good deeds.

JESUS ESCAPES DEATH — Jesus tells the people that God is displeased by their sins. Some of them become angry and try to stone Him, but He passes right through them.

JESUS SPEAKS FROM A BOAT — So many people come to hear Jesus speak that they almost crush Him. He gets into a boat and continues speaking about God to them.

JESUS URGES KINDNESS — Jesus wants us to be kind to everyone. If we hurt anyone, we must tell him we are sorry. This will please God.

THE MIRACULOUS CATCH OF FISH — One day Jesus tells Peter to row to the middle of the lake to fish. Peter obeys although he had fished all night and caught nothing. He catches so many fish that his boat almost sinks.

JESUS CURES A PARALYTIC — Some men bring a paralyzed man to Jesus. Because of their faith, Jesus forgives the man his sins and then cures him completely.

JESUS AND THE ROMAN OFFICER — A Roman officer has faith that Jesus can cure his sick servant boy even from a distance. Jesus praises the man's faith and cures his servant.

JESUS RAISES A WIDOW'S SON — Jesus meets a funeral procession for the only son of a widow. He feels sorry for the mother and brings her son back to life.

JESUS TELLS US GOD IS GOOD — Jesus tells His disciples how God feeds the birds and how beautiful He makes lilies. He shows that God will take care of us too.

JESUS CURES A BLIND MAN — A blind man hears that Jesus is passing by and cries out to be helped. Jesus stops and gives him sight because of his faith.

JESUS SPEAKS OF THE FATHER — Jesus tells His disciples about God the Father. He wants all people to know that the Father is powerful and good.

MIRACLE OF THE LOAVES — Those who have come to hear Jesus are hungry and have no food. Jesus blesses five loaves and two fish, and feeds over 5,000 people.

JESUS CALMS THE STORM — Jesus is in a boat that is in danger of sinking because of a storm. He tells the winds to be still, and there is a great calm.

TRUE HAPPINESS — Jesus talks to the people about true happiness. We must be poor in spirit and at peace with one another. Above all, we must love God.

JESUS APPEARS IN GLORY — Peter, James, and John see Jesus in glory with Moses and Elijah. They hear a voice from heaven saying, "This is My beloved Son. Listen to Him."

JESUS CURES A DEAF-MUTE — A man who cannot hear or speak comes to Jesus. Jesus puts His fingers in his ears, touches his tongue, and says, "Be opened." The man is cured.

PRAISE OF MARY — A woman praises Jesus' Mother. Jesus remembers how Mary always obeyed God. He says that all who obey God as she did are His brother, sister, and mother.

JESUS CURES A SICK BOY — A royal official begs Jesus to come and cure his sick son. Jesus says, "Go home. Your son lives." At that moment the boy is cured.

JESUS RAISES A DEAD GIRL — The young daughter of Jairus is dead. Jesus goes to her, takes her hand, and says, "Little girl, get up." She rises and begins to walk around.

JESUS CURES TEN LEPERS — Jesus cures ten lepers by sending them to the priest. Only one comes back to give Him thanks. We should always thank Jesus for His goodness to us.

JESUS' DEATH AND RESURRECTION — Jesus tells His disciples that He will suffer, be put to death, and rise on the third day. He will go through all this to save the faithful.

THE PEOPLE PRAISE JESUS — Jesus rides into Jerusalem on a donkey. The people wave palm branches and shout, "Blessed is He Who comes in the name of the Lord."

JESUS CLEANSES THE TEMPLE — Jesus finds merchants and money-changers in the Temple, His Father's house. He drives them out, saying, "My house is a house of prayer."

JESUS WEEPS OVER THE CITY — Jesus weeps over Jerusalem because its people did not accept the Prophets or Him. As a result, the city will be destroyed by their enemies.

THE LAST SUPPER — The night before His Death, Jesus changes bread and wine into His Body and Blood. He tells the disciples to do the same thing in remembrance of Him.

THE SPIRIT OF JESUS — Jesus tells His disciples He is returning to the Father Who sent Him. He will send them the Holy Spirit to take His place and help them always.

AGONY IN THE GARDEN — Jesus and His disciples go to the Garden of Gethsemane. He prays that His suffering might not happen, yet He will do the Father's will.

JESUS IS SENTENCED TO DEATH — Jesus is brought before the Roman governor and sentenced to death, even though He has done no wrong. He accepts His sentence in order to save us.

DEATH OF JESUS — After being beaten, Jesus is nailed to a cross. His Mother and John the disciple stand by Him. After three hours of terrible pain, He dies and wins salvation for the faithful.

RESURRECTION OF JESUS — On the third day after His Death, Jesus rises and enters into His glory. We too will rise with Him to glory, provided we follow Him by our lives.

APPEARANCE OF THE RISEN JESUS — Jesus appears to the Apostles, but Thomas is absent and refuses to believe. Jesus returns and tells Thomas to touch His wounds. Thomas says, "My Lord and my God."

"FEED MY SHEEP." — After His Resurrection, Jesus tells Peter, "Feed My sheep." In so doing, He calls Peter to uphold his brothers and sisters in faith as the first Pope.

ASCENSION OF JESUS — Jesus spends forty days with His disciples after His Resurrection, teaching them many things. Then He returns to His Father to await them in heaven.

THE MIRACLES OF JESUS

Water Made Wine at Cana

The Royal Official's Son

The Great Number of Fish

The Cure of a Possessed Man

Peter's Mother-in-Law

Healing a Leper

Healing a Paralyzed Man

The Cure on the Sabbath

Healing the Withered Hand

The Centurion's Servant

The Widow's Son

The Blind and Mute Man

The Calming of the Storm

Jesus Expels Demons

Raising the Daughter of Jairus

The Suffering Woman

Two Blind Men

The Mute Demoniac

Five Thousand Fed
Jesus Walks on the Water
A Gentile Woman's Faith
A Deaf and Mute Man
Four Thousand Fed
The Blind Man at Bethsaida
A Possessed Boy
Jesus Pays the Temple Tax
The Man Born Blind
The Lame, Blind, and Mute
The Crippled Woman
The Raising of Lazarus
The Man with Dropsy
The Ten Lepers
The Blind at Jericho
The Withered Fig Tree
Jesus Heals the Servant's Ear
The Great Catch of Fish

THE PRINCIPAL PARABLES OF JESUS

The Indecisive Children

The Two Debtors

The Fig Tree

The Barren Fig Tree

The Persistent Widow

A Divided Kingdom

The Workers in the Vineyard

The Unmerciful Servant

The Mustard Seed and the Yeast

The Net

The Pharisee and the Tax Collector

The Rich Man and Lazarus

The Rich Fool

The Good Samaritan

The Ambitious Guest

The Sower

The Secretly Growing Seed

The Faithful Servant

The Unprofitable Servants

The Lost Sheep

The Good Shepherd

The Talents

The Lost (or Prodigal) Son

The Two Sons

The Ten Gold Coins

The Tenants

The Hidden Treasure and the Pearl

The Owner of the House

Union with Jesus

The Wedding Banquet/The Great Supper

The Weeds

The Dishonest Steward

PRAYERS

The Sign of the Cross

IN the name of the Father,
and of the Son,
and of the Holy Spirit.
Amen.

The Glory Be

GLORY be to the Father,
and to the Son,
and to the Holy Spirit.

As it was in the beginning,
is now,
and ever shall be,
world without end.
Amen.

Prayers on Awaking

O MY God,
I offer You
through the Immaculate Heart of Mary
all my thoughts, words, actions, and sufferings of this day.
I offer them
to please You, to honor You,
and to make up for my sins.
Sweet Mother Mary,
keep me in your care.

THANK You, O God,
for this new day.
Help me in body and soul,
in my work and play.
Bless all I do or think or say.
Let me do everything to please You,
and to keep me from all danger and sin.

The Our Father

OUR Father, Who art in heaven,
hallowed be Thy name;
Thy kingdom come,
Thy will be done
on earth as it is in heaven.
Give us this day our daily bread,
and forgive us our trespasses,
as we forgive those who trespass against us;
and lead us not into temptation,
but deliver us from evil.
Amen.

The Apostles' Creed

I BELIEVE in God, the Father Almighty, Creator of heaven and earth, and in Jesus Christ, His only Son, Our Lord, Who was conceived by the Holy Spirit, born of the Virgin Mary, suffered under Pontius Pilate, was crucified, died and was buried; He descended into hell; on the third day He rose again from the dead; He ascended into heaven, and is seated at the right hand of God the Father Almighty; from there He will come to judge the living and the dead.

I believe in the Holy Spirit, the Holy catholic Church, the communion of saints, the forgiveness of sins, the resurrection of the body, and life everlasting. Amen.

Act of Faith

MY God, I believe in You, because You are the eternal truth. Help me to accept Your word and always remember that You love me and care for me. I believe in all that Your Catholic Church teaches.

Act of Hope

MY God, I hope in You, because in Jesus Christ, Your Son, You have promised me Your love forever. You will never leave me, if only I stay away from sin and remain with You.

Act of Love

O MY God, I love You, because You are the Greatest Good and deserve all my love, as my Creator and my Father. I love all people because You want me to love them for they are Your children too.

The Hail Mary

HAIL, Mary, full of grace!
The Lord is with you;
blessed are you among women,
and blessed is the fruit of your womb,
Jesus.

Holy Mary, Mother of God,
pray for us sinners,
now and at the hour of our death.
Amen.

Prayer to My Guardian Angel

ANGEL of God,
my Guardian dear,
God's love for me
has sent you here.

Ever this day
be at my side,
to light and guard,
to rule and guide.

My dear Guardian Angel,
teach me to know God,
to love and serve Him
and save my soul.

Keep me from all danger,
and lead me to heaven.

Act of Contrition

O MY God, I am heartily sorry
for having offended You.
I detest all my sins,
because of Your just punishment.

But most of all,
because they offend You, my God,
Who are all good
and deserving of all my love.

I firmly resolve,
with the help of Your grace,
to sin no more
and to avoid the near occasions of sin.
Amen.

Prayer for Mercy

GOD,
be merciful to me,
a sinner.

Grace before Meals

BLESS us, O Lord,
and these Your gifts,
which we are about to receive
from Your goodness,
through Christ our Lord.
Amen.

Grace after Meals

WE thank You, O God,
for all these gifts,
which we have received from Your goodness,
through Christ our Lord.
Amen.

Prayer of Thanksgiving

GIVE thanks to the Lord,
for He is good;
His kindness endures forever.

Hail, Holy Queen

HAIL, Holy Queen, Mother of Mercy;
hail our life, our sweetness, and our hope.

To you do we cry,
poor banished children of Eve.

To you do we send up our sighs,
mourning and weeping
in this vale of tears.

Turn then, most gracious advocate,
your eyes of mercy toward us.

And after this, our exile,
show unto us the blessed fruit
of your womb, Jesus.

O clement, O loving,
O sweet Virgin Mary.

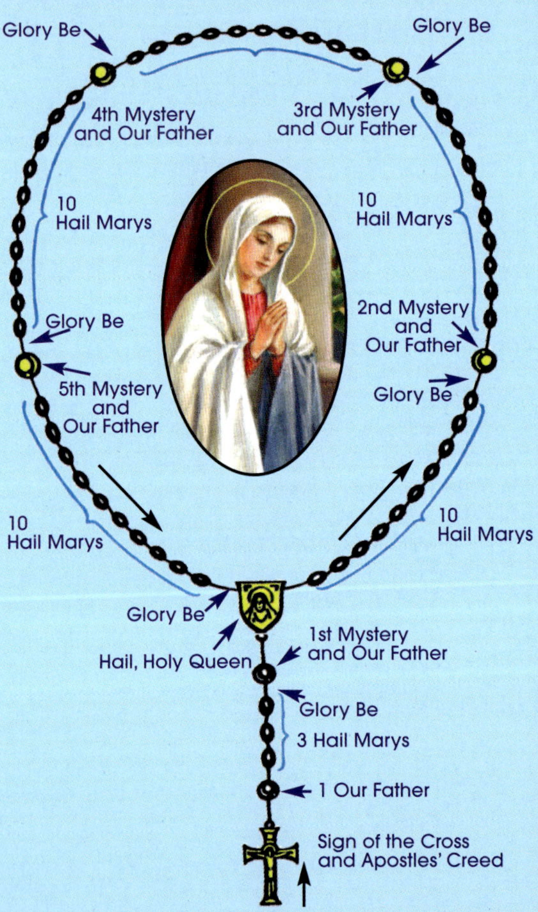
Glory Be
Glory Be
4th Mystery and Our Father
3rd Mystery and Our Father
10 Hail Marys
10 Hail Marys
Glory Be
2nd Mystery and Our Father
5th Mystery and Our Father
Glory Be
10 Hail Marys
10 Hail Marys
Glory Be
Hail, Holy Queen
1st Mystery and Our Father
Glory Be
3 Hail Marys
1 Our Father
Sign of the Cross and Apostles' Creed

THE HOLY ROSARY

THE Rosary calls to mind the most important events in the lives of Jesus and Mary. These events are called Mysteries and are divided into the following 4 groups.

The JOYFUL MYSTERIES help us to think of Mary's joy when Jesus came into the world.

The LUMINOUS MYSTERIES help us to think of Mary's joy when Jesus began to proclaim the Good News of salvation for all who followed Him.

The SORROWFUL MYSTERIES help us to think of Mary's great sorrow when Jesus suffered for our salvation.

The GLORIOUS MYSTERIES help us to think of the glorious Resurrection of Jesus and the Crowning of Mary as Queen of Heaven.

HOW TO SAY THE ROSARY

Say the Apostles' Creed.

Say 1 Our Father.

Say 3 Hail Marys.

Say 1 Glory Be, then announce the 1st Mystery and say 1 Our Father.

Say 10 Hail Marys.

Announce the 2nd Mystery and continue in the same way until each of the 5 Mysteries is said.

The Five Joyful Mysteries

3. The Birth of Jesus
Jesus, You are born in a stable. May I value grace above money.

1. The Annunciation to Mary
Mary, Jesus will be your Son. Teach me to love Him.

4. The Presentation
Jesus, You are offered to God in the Temple. Help me to obey.

2. The Visitation
Mary, you visit your cousin Elizabeth. Help me to be kind.

5. The Finding in the Temple
Jesus, You are found with the teachers. Give me true wisdom.

*The Five Luminous Mysteries**

* They are reprinted here from our Picture Book *The Holy Rosary,* which in 2004 received the Imprimatur from Most Rev. Frank J. Rodimer, Bishop of Paterson.

1. The Baptism of Jesus
Jesus, You rejoiced at Your Baptism. Help me to keep my baptismal promises.

2. Christ's Miracle at Cana
Jesus, You revealed Yourself at Cana. Help me to do all that You ask.

3. Proclamation of the Kingdom
Jesus, You called people to repent. Help me to seek forgiveness.

4. The Transfiguration
Jesus, You showed Your glory. Help me to become a new person.

5. Institution of the Eucharist
Jesus, You gave us the Eucharist. Help me to participate at Mass.

The Five Sorrowful Mysteries

1. Agony in the Garden
Jesus, You are saddened by my sins. Give me true sorrow.

2. The Scourging at the Pillar
Jesus, You are whipped by the soldiers. Help me to be pure.

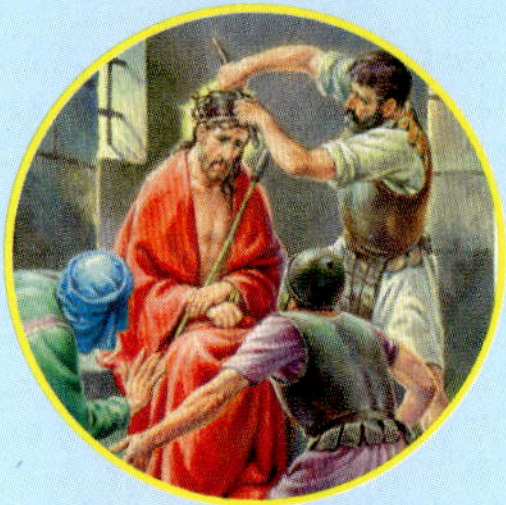

3. The Crowning with Thorns
Jesus, You receive a crown of thorns. Give me true courage.

4. The Carrying of the Cross
Jesus, You carry the Cross gladly. Help me to be patient.

5. The Crucifixion
Jesus, You die on the Cross for me. Keep me in Your grace.

The Five Glorious Mysteries

1. The Resurrection
Jesus, You rise from Your tomb. Help me to believe in You.

2. The Ascension
Jesus, You go to Your Father in Heaven. Help me to hope in You.

3. Descent of the Holy Spirit
Holy Spirit, You come to bring grace. Help me to love God.

4. The Assumption of Mary
Mary, you are taken to heaven. Let me be devoted to you.

5. The Crowning of Mary
Mary, you are crowned Queen of Heaven. Let me serve you.

STATIONS *of the* CROSS

1. Jesus Is Condemned to Death

O Jesus, help me to appreciate Your sanctifying grace more and more.

2. Jesus Bears His Cross

O Jesus, You chose to die for me. Help me to love You always with all my heart.

3. Jesus Falls the First Time

O Jesus, make me strong to conquer my wicked passions, and to rise quickly from sin.

4. Jesus Meets His Mother

O Jesus, grant me a tender love for Your Mother, who offered You for love of me.

STATIONS *of the* CROSS

5. Jesus Is Helped by Simon

O Jesus, like Simon, lead me ever closer to You through my daily crosses and trials.

6. Jesus and Veronica

O Jesus, imprint Your image on my heart that I may be faithful to You all my life.

7. Jesus Falls a Second Time

O Jesus, I repent for having offended You. Grant me forgiveness of all my sins.

8. Jesus Speaks to the Women

O Jesus, grant me tears of compassion for Your sufferings and of sorrow for my sins.

STATIONS *of the* CROSS

9. Jesus Falls a Third Time

O Jesus, let me never yield to despair. Let me come to You in hardship and spiritual distress.

10. He Is Stripped of His Garments

O Jesus, let me sacrifice all my attachments rather than imperil the divine life of my soul.

11. Jesus Is Nailed to the Cross

O Jesus, strengthen my faith and increase my love for You. Help me to accept my crosses.

12. Jesus Dies on the Cross

O Jesus, I thank You for making me a child of God. Help me to forgive others.

STATIONS *of the* CROSS

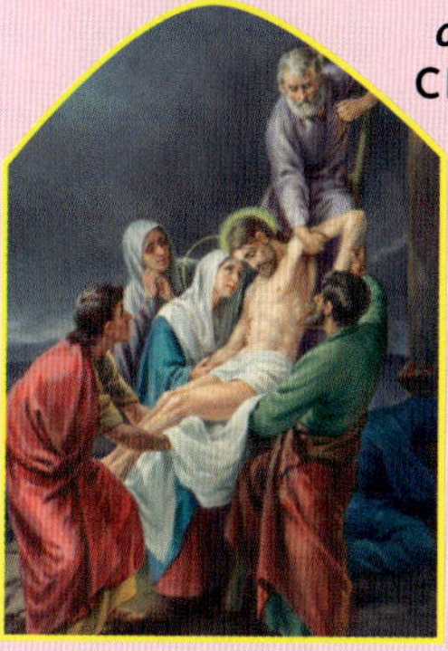

13. Jesus Is Taken Down from the Cross

O Jesus, through the intercession of Your holy Mother, let me be pleasing to You.

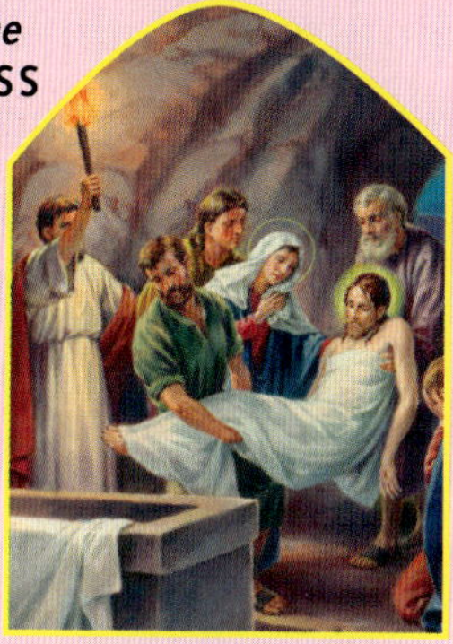

14. Jesus Is Laid in the Tomb

O Jesus, strengthen my will to live for You on earth and bring me to eternal bliss in heaven.

Prayer after the Stations

JESUS, You became an example of humility, obedience and patience, and preceded me on the way of life bearing Your Cross. Grant that, inflamed with Your love, I may cheerfully take upon myself the sweet yoke of Your Gospel together with the mortification of the Cross and follow You as a true disciple so that I may be united with You in heaven. Amen.

COMMUNION PRAYERS

BEFORE HOLY COMMUNION

An Act of Offering

Dear Jesus, with this Holy Communion, I offer You today, my thoughts, my words, and all that I do. May Your grace help me to be always ready to receive You.

An Act of Faith

O good Jesus, You are now on the altar. I believe that You are the same God Who made heaven and earth, and Who became a child like me to draw us all close to You. I believe that now You are really present in Holy Communion to be the Food of our souls. I believe it all because You said so.

An Act of Hope

O good Jesus, You come to me with the riches of heaven and earth. I truly hope that You will bring me all the help I need to serve You well and to get to heaven.

An Act of Love

Dear Jesus, how much I should love You, after all that You have suffered for me. Make me grow more and more in love for You. How happy I shall be when in a few moments I shall hold You close to my heart.

An Act of Contrition

I know, dear Jesus, I have often offended You by my sins. But I am very sorry now. One word from Your holy lips, and my soul will be whiter than snow. I promise, dear Jesus, to be very careful not to offend You again.

An Act of Adoration

My Lord and my God, I believe that You are really present in the Blessed Sacrament. I adore You, O Jesus, my Creator, my Lord, my Redeemer, my Love.

Come, dear Jesus, come into my heart. I am going to receive You in Holy Communion. You are God.

My Lord and my God!

Thank You, Jesus, for Coming to Me

Dear Jesus, Your miracles are very great. Your greatest miracle is that of giving Your Body and Blood to us in Holy Communion. This is You Yourself and not just bread.

I thank You for giving Yourself to me. May this Holy Communion bring me closer to You, my Lord and my God.

Acts of Faith, Hope, Love, Petition

O good Jesus, You are King of heaven and earth. I believe in You. I hope in You. I love You.

O Jesus, I have just eaten You as Food for my soul. You are God's Gift to me to help me imitate You. There are many things I need from You so I may do what You want me to.

Help me especially to love my family, my friends, everyone, as You love them. I forgive anyone who has ever done wrong to me. Help me to love my enemies and do good to everyone, even those who hurt me. Jesus, for You I live; for You I die; I wish to be Yours forever.

An Act of Joy

May my soul always want You, O dear Jesus.

May You always be with us in Holy Communion.

May You live in my heart always.

May Your many graces help me to be happy with You forever in heaven.

An Act of Offering

O Jesus, You have given Yourself to me; now let me give myself to You.

I give You my body, that it may be chaste and pure. I give You my soul, that it may be free from sin. I give You my heart, that it may always love You.

I give You every thought, word, and deed of my life, and I offer all for Your honor and glory.

THE SACRAMENT OF PENANCE

To receive the Sacrament of Penance worthily, I must:

1. **Remember my sins.**
2. **Be sorry for my sins.**
3. **Make up my mind not to sin again.**
4. **Tell my sins to the Priest.**
5. **Do the penance the Priest gives me.**

Preparation for Confession

Did I commit any of these sins?

The Ten Commandments of God

GOD

1. I, the Lord, am your God. You shall not have other gods besides Me.

Did I miss my morning or night prayers?

Did I misbehave during Mass?

HOLY NAME

2. You shall not take the name of the Lord, your God, in vain.

Did I use holy names, like "Jesus" and "God" when I should not have used them?

SUNDAY

3. Remember to keep holy the Lord's day.

Did I miss Mass through my own fault on Sunday or Holydays?

PARENTS

4. Honor your father and your mother.

Did I disobey my parents or teachers?

Was I mean to them?

Did I answer back?

Did I make fun of my parents or the elderly?

BE KIND

5. You shall not kill.

Did I hate anyone?

Did I do anything mean to anyone?

Did I let myself get angry?

Did I call anyone bad names?

Did I quarrel and fight?

Did I wish anything bad for anyone?

Did I make anyone sin?

BE PURE

6. You shall not commit adultery.

9. You shall not covet your neighbor's wife.

Did I do anything that was really impure?

Was it alone or with others?

Did I willingly keep impure thoughts in my mind?

Did I sin by using impure words?

Did I sin by looking at or reading anything impure?

Did I sin by talking about or listening to anything impure?

BE HONEST

7. You shall not steal.

10. You shall not covet anything that belongs to your neighbor.

Did I steal anything?

Did I keep anything that did not belong to me?

Did I damage what belongs to someone else?

BE TRUTHFUL

8. You shall not bear false witness against your neighbor.

Did I tell any lies?

Did I say mean things about anyone?

Did I like to listen to unkind talk about others?

Pray the Act of Contrition on page 101.

IMPORTANT TEACHINGS

THE BEATITUDES

1. Blessed are the poor in spirit, for theirs is the kingdom of heaven.
2. Blessed are those who mourn, for they shall be comforted.
3. Blessed are the meek, for they shall inherit the earth.
4. Blessed are those who hunger and thirst for righteousness, for they shall be satisfied.
5. Blessed are the merciful, for they shall obtain mercy.
6. Blessed are the pure in heart, for they shall see God.
7. Blessed are the peacemakers, for they shall be called the children of God.
8. Blessed are those who suffer for righteousness' sake, for theirs is the kingdom of heaven.

THE SACRAMENTS

Baptism

Christ gives us a new life: the life of grace in His Church. We celebrate our birth to faith, as children of God, and we die to sin.

Penance: Reconciliation

Christ forgives our sins and restores or increases our grace. We celebrate our conversion and reconciliation with God and the Church.

Holy Eucharist

We celebrate the Lord's Passover, the sacrifice of the Cross. Christ feeds us with the Bread of Life, His Body and Blood.

Confirmation

Christ strengthens us as Christians and He makes us His soldiers and apostles to defend and spread the faith.

Anointing of the Sick

Christ strengthens our soul in the face of sickness and death. We celebrate the Christian hope in life eternal.

Holy Orders

Christ consecrates His ministers for the Priestly Service of the People of God.

Matrimony

Christ sanctifies the unbreakable union of man and woman in mutual love and support, to have children and to bring them up in the Catholic faith.

HOLYDAYS OF OBLIGATION

THE IMMACULATE CONCEPTION
December 8

This day we celebrate that Mary was sinless from the moment she was conceived.

THE NATIVITY OF THE LORD
December 25

This is the birthday of Jesus, Our Savior, in Bethlehem.

MARY, THE HOLY MOTHER OF GOD
January 1

We recall that Mary gave birth to Jesus, God the Son.

IN THE DIOCESES OF THE UNITED STATES

THE ASCENSION
(40 days after Easter)

On this day, Jesus returned to His Father in heaven.

THE ASSUMPTION
August 15

We recall that the Blessed Virgin Mary was taken up to heaven.

ALL SAINTS
November 1

This day we celebrate all the Saints that have gone to heaven.

The Church Year and Vestment Colors

Advent: The Church Year begins on the First Sunday of Advent. There are four Sundays in Advent. The Priest wears **violet**. It is a time to prepare for Jesus' Birth on Christmas.

Christmas Time: This begins with the Vigil Masses on Christmas Eve and ends on the Feast of the Baptism of the Lord. The Priest wears white. It is a time to celebrate Jesus coming into the world.

Lent: This time of prayer, fasting, and good deeds extends from Ash Wednesday to the beginning of the Sacred Paschal Triduum. The Priest wears **violet** most of this time (although he wears white on Holy Thursday and **red** on Good Friday and Palm Sunday).

Easter Time: This is a 50-day celebration of Jesus' Resurrection and His sending of the Holy Spirit. The Priest wears white, except on Pentecost (when he wears **red**), the close of Easter Time.

Ordinary Time: This occurs twice in a year: from the end of Christmas Time to the beginning of Lent and from after Pentecost until the Solemnity of Christ the King, the last Sunday in the Church Year. The Priest wears **green**. During this time, we recall Jesus' works and teachings.

PRAYER BEFORE A CRUCIFIX

LOOK down on me,
good and gentle
Jesus.

Make my soul
strong in faith,
hope and love.

Make me really sorry
for my sins
so I will never sin
again.

I am sad when I see the wounds
on Your hands and feet,
and think of the words
of Your Prophet David:

'They have pierced my hands and feet,
they have hurt all my bones."